Friendship Love AND Laughter

INSPIRATIONAL
QUOTES
TO LIVE BY

Bob Phillips

HARVEST HOUSE PUBLISHERS
EUGENE, OREGON 97402

FRIENDSHIP, LOVE, & LAUGHTER

Copyright © 1993 by Harvest House Publishers
Eugene, Oregon 97402

Friendship, love & laughter / [compiled by] Bob Phillips.
        p.   cm.
    ISBN 1-56507-038-0
    1. Friendship—Quotations, maxims, etc.   2. Laughter—
Quotations, maxims, etc.   3. Love—Quotations, maxims,
etc.   I. Phillips, Bob, 1940–
PN6084.F8F59   1993   92-26893
                                                                         CIP

Printed in the United States of America.

It has been said that
you only keep what you give away.
Friendship, love and laughter
need to be given away.

To have friends,
one must give themselves in friendship.

The deepest experience of love
is found when we impart
love to others.

Laughter,
when shared with friends and loved ones,
brings zest, gusto and delight.

Bob Phillips
Hume Lake, CA

*I am wealthy
in my friends.*

—William Shakespeare

Friendship, Love & Laughter

*To love
is to choose.*

—French proverb

Friendship, Love & Laughter

A good laugh
is sunshine in a house.

—William Thackeray

*Some of my best friends
are children. In fact,
all of my best friends
are children.*

—J.D. Salinger

Friendship, Love & Laughter

You can make more friends in two months by becoming interested in other people than you can in two years by trying to get other people interested in you.

—Dale Carnegie

Friendship, Love & Laughter

They do not love
that do not show
their love.

Friendship, Love & Laughter

The best way to cheer yourself up is to try to cheer somebody else up.

—Mark Twain

Friendship, Love & Laughter

Love
at first sight
never happens
before breakfast.

Friendship, Love & Laughter

*A mirror
reflects a man's face, but
what he is really like is
shown by the kind of
friends he chooses.*

—Proverbs 27:19

Friendship, Love & Laughter

*Who,
being loved,
is poor?*

—Oscar Wilde

Friendship, Love & Laughter

*It's smart
to pick your friends
—but not to pieces.*

Friendship, Love & Laughter

*Love is a
little foolishness
and a lot of
curiosity.*

Friendship, Love & Laughter

*Even though
you are miles away,
there are always two cups
on my table.*

*The supreme happiness of
life is the conviction
that we are loved.*

—Victor Hugo

*Laughter is not a
bad beginning for a
friendship, and it is the
best ending for one.*

—Oscar Wilde

A merry heart does good,
like medicine.

—Proverbs 17:22 (NKJV)

Friendship, Love & Laughter

Friends are made
by many acts
—and lost by only one.

Friendship, Love & Laughter

*To love is to
place our happiness
in the happiness
of another.*

—Gottfried Wilhelm
von Leibniz

Friendship, Love & Laughter

A good laugh is a mighty good thing, and rather too scarce a good thing.

—Herman Melville

*Laughter appears
to stand in need of
an echo.*

—Henri Bergson

*A valuable friend
is one who'll tell you
what you should be told,
even if it offends you.*

—Frank A. Clark

Friendship, Love & Laughter

*You will find as you look
back upon your life that
the moments when you
have really lived are the
moments when you have
done things in the
spirit of love.*

—Henry Drummond

Friendship, Love & Laughter

*The sign of wisdom is a
continual cheerfulness.*

—French proverb

*Love is a
grave mental illness.*

—Plato

Friendship, Love & Laughter

*Correct
your friend secretly
and praise him
publicly.*

Friendship, Love & Laughter

Love is very patient and kind, never jealous or envious, never boastful or proud, never haughty or selfish or rude.

—1 Corinthians 13:4,5

Friendship, Love & Laughter

*He who has the courage to
laugh is almost as much
the master of the world as
he who is ready to die.*

—Giacomo Leopardi

Friendship, Love & Laughter

There is always a secret irritation about a laugh in which we cannot join.

—Agnes Repplier

Friendship, Love & Laughter

*There are not many things
in life so beautiful
as true friendship,
and not many things
more uncommon.*

*An old man in love is like
a flower in winter.*

—Portuguese proverb

Friendship, Love & Laughter

*The first sigh
of love is the
last of wisdom.*

—Antoine Bret

*Before borrowing
money from a friend,
decide which you
need most.*

Friendship, Love & Laughter

Friendship,
of itself a holy tie,
is made more sacred
by adversity.

—John Dryden

Friendship, Love & Laughter

Love is a fabric which never fades, no matter how often it is washed in the water of adversity and grief.

Friendship, Love & Laughter

Do not use a hatchet to remove a fly from your friend's forehead.

*Love is blind,
and marriage is an
eye-opener.*

*I no doubt
deserved my enemies,
but I don't believe
I deserved my friends.*

—Walt Whitman

Friendship, Love & Laughter

Love sought is good,
but given unsought
is better.

—William Shakespeare

Friendship, Love & Laughter

*Strange, when you come
to think of it, that of all the
countless folk who have
lived before our time on
this planet, not one is
known in history or in
legend as having died
of laughter.*

—Max Beerbohm

Friendship, Love & Laughter

*Love may not make the
world spin around, but it
certainly makes a lot of
people dizzy.*

Friendship, Love & Laughter

A friend is a person with whom you dare to be yourself.

Friendship, Love & Laughter

*Whom we love best,
to them we can
say least.*

Friendship, Love & Laughter

*What a wonderful life
I've had! I only wish
I'd realized it sooner.*

—Colette

Friendship, Love & Laughter

*Love is a softening
of the hearteries.*

Friendship, Love & Laughter

Friendship
is like a bank account.
You can't continue to
draw on it without
making deposits.

Friendship, Love & Laughter

If you love somebody,
tell them.

—Rod McKuen

Friendship, Love & Laughter

I love making friends—
it's people I can't stand!

—Linus

Friendship, Love & Laughter

Love is a cough
that cannot be hid.

—George Herbert

*A friend
must not be injured,
even in jest.*

—Publilius Syrus

Friendship, Love & Laughter

*A new commandment
I give unto you, that you
love one another.*

—Jesus Christ

Friendship, Love & Laughter

*Mirth is
God's medicine.*

—Henry Ward Beecher

Friendship, Love & Laughter

*Familiarity
breeds contempt—
and children.*

—Mark Twain

Friendship, Love & Laughter

*One should go invited
to a friend in good fortune
and uninvited in misfortune.*

—Swedish proverb

Friendship, Love & Laughter

Love does not die easily.
It is a living thing.
It thrives in the face
of all life's hazards,
save one—neglect.

—James Bryden

Friendship, Love & Laughter

*Love is a smoke
raised with the fume
of sighs.*

—William Shakespeare

Friendship, Love & Laughter

Love arrives on tiptoe
and bangs the door
when it leaves.

—Robert Lembke

He who seeks friends
without faults
stays forever
without friends.

Friendship, Love & Laughter

*Love
is the greatest
refreshment in life.*

—Pablo Picasso

Friendship, Love & Laughter

*If Jack's in love,
he's no judge of
Jill's beauty.*

—Benjamin Franklin

*Love teaches
donkeys to dance.*

—French proverb

Friendship, Love & Laughter

*Good company
in a journey makes
the way seem shorter.*

—Izaak Walton

*The course of true love
never did run smooth.*

—William Shakespeare

Friendship, Love & Laughter

Good humor makes all things tolerable.

—Henry Ward Beecher

What is irritating about love is that it is a crime that requires an accomplice.

—C. Baudelaire

Friendship, Love & Laughter

*A true friend
is one soul in two bodies.*

—Aristotle

Friendship, Love & Laughter

*The way
to love anything
is to realize that it
may be lost.*

—G.K. Chesterton

The love
of truth lies at the root
of much humor.

Friendship, Love & Laughter

*No man ever
distinguished himself
who could not bear
to be laughed at.*

—Maria Edgeworth

*Go often
to the house of your friend,
for weeds soon choke up
the unused path.*

—William Shakespeare

Friendship, Love & Laughter

*Life has taught us
that love does not consist
in gazing at each other,
but in looking outward
together in the same
direction.*

—Antoine de Saint Exupery

Friendship, Love & Laughter

*Instead of
loving your enemies,
treat your friends
a little better.*

—Ed Howe

*He who falls in love
meets a worse fate
than he who leaps
from a rock.*

—Latin proverb

Friendship, Love & Laughter

*One friend
in a lifetime is much;
two are many;
three are hardly possible.*

—Henry Adams

Friendship, Love & Laughter

*Love cures people—
both the ones who give it
and the ones who receive it.*

—Dr. Karl Menninger

Friendship, Love & Laughter

I exhort you
to be of good cheer.

—Acts 27:22 (KJV)

Friendship, Love & Laughter

*Happiness?
That's nothing more
than health and a
poor memory.*

—Albert Schweitzer

Friendship, Love & Laughter

*One should
keep his friendships
in constant repair.*

—Samuel Johnson

*He drew a circle that
shut me out,
but love and I had the
wit to win,
we drew a larger circle
that took him in.*

Friendship, Love & Laughter

*A cheerful look
makes a dish a feast.*

—George Herbert

*Sudden love
takes the longest time
to be cured.*

—Jean de LaBruyere

*Just as yellow gold
is tested in the fire,
so is friendship to be
tested by adversity.*

—Ovid

Friendship, Love & Laughter

Better a meal of vegetables where there is love than a fattened calf with hatred.

—Proverbs 15:17 (NIV)

Friendship, Love & Laughter

*Cheerfulness is the
offshoot of goodness.*

—Christian Nestell Bovee

Friendship, Love & Laughter

*Love maketh
a wit of a fool.*

*Life is to be fortified
by many friendships.
To love, and to be loved,
is the greatest happiness
of existence.*

—Sydney Smith

Friendship, Love & Laughter

*What's so remarkable
about love at first sight?
It's when people have been
looking at each other
for years that it
becomes remarkable.*

Friendship, Love & Laughter

*With the fearful strain
that is on me night and day,
if I did not laugh I should die.*

—Abraham Lincoln

*Love never dies
of starvation,
but often of indigestion.*

—French proverb

Friendship
is a sheltering tree.

Friendship, Love & Laughter

*For God
so loved the world,
that he gave his only
begotten Son, that
whosoever
believeth in him
should not perish,
but have everlasting life.*

—John 3:16 (KJV)

Friendship, Love & Laughter

*Let us
be of good cheer,
remembering
that the misfortunes
hardest to bear
are those which
never happen.*

—Lowell

Friendship, Love & Laughter

*We are all
here for a spell;
get all the good laughs
you can.*

—Will Rogers

*He is my friend because
we have so many faults
in common.*

Friendship, Love & Laughter

*The heart
has its reasons
which reason does not
understand.*

—Blaise Pascal

Friendship, Love & Laughter

*One good laugh
destroys a hundred cares.*

Friendship, Love & Laughter

*Love, like a chicken salad
or restaurant hash, must
be taken with blind faith
or it loses its flavor.*

—Helen Rowland

Friendship, Love & Laughter

*Treat your friends
as you do your pictures,
and place them in their
best light.*

—Jennie Jerome Churchill

Friendship, Love & Laughter

If you love someone you will be loyal to him no matter what the cost. You will always believe in him, always expect the best of him, and always stand your ground in defending him.

—1 Corinthians 13:7

Friendship, Love & Laughter

*Laughter is a
powerful force that
keeps us from becoming
a negative person.*

—R.E. Phillips

Friendship, Love & Laughter

We don't believe in rheumatism and true love until after the first attack.

—Marie von Eber-Eschenbach

Friendship, Love & Laughter

*So long as we are
loved by others
I should say that we are
almost indispensable;
and no man is useless
while he has a friend.*

—Robert Louis Stevenson

Friendship, Love & Laughter

*To love and win
is the best thing;
to love and lose the next best.*

—William Thackeray

*Laughter
makes the hours
seem short.*

Friendship, Love & Laughter

*If only
one could tell true love
from false love
as one can tell mushrooms
from toadstools.*

—Katherine Mansfield

*Iron sharpens iron;
so a man sharpens the
countenance of his friend.*

—Proverbs 27:17 (NKJV)

Friendship, Love & Laughter

*Love
is friendship
set on fire.*

—Jeremy Taylor

Friendship, Love & Laughter

*Keep company
with the more cheerful
sort of the godly;
there is no mirth
like the mirth of believers.*

—Richard Baxter

Friendship, Love & Laughter

*Nothing spoils
the taste of peanut butter
like unrequited love.*

—Charlie Brown

Friendship, Love & Laughter

*True friendship
is a plant of low growth,
and must undergo
and withstand
the shocks of adversity
before it is entitled
to the appellation.*

—George Washington

Friendship, Love & Laughter

*Love
will always find a way
to be practical.*

—Joe White

Friendship, Love & Laughter

*Laughter
is the sensation of
feeling good all over,
and showing it
principally in one place.*

—Josh Billings

*Happiness is a perfume
which you can't
pour on someone
without getting some
on yourself.*

—Ralph Waldo Emerson

Friendship, Love & Laughter

Love is blind;
friendship closes its eyes.

Friendship, Love & Laughter

*Love covers
a multitude of sins.*

—1 Peter 4:8 (NIV)

Friendship, Love & Laughter

Friendship is of so sweet and steady and loyal and enduring a nature that it will last through a whole lifetime, if not asked to lend money.

—Mark Twain

Friendship, Love & Laughter

*Love
is like a game of chess.
One false move and
you're mated.*

Friendship, Love & Laughter

*Friendship may,
and often does,
grow into love;
but love never subsides
into friendship.*

—Lord Byron

Friendship, Love & Laughter

*In life,
actions speak
louder than words,
but in love, the eyes do.*

—Susan B. Anthony

Friendship, Love & Laughter

*Laughter
is the shortest distance
between two people.*

—Victor Borge

Friendship, Love & Laughter

*Love
is a state of mind
which has nothing to do
with the mind.*

Friendship, Love & Laughter

*He who wants
a long friendship
should keep a
short memory.*

Friendship, Love & Laughter

*To love
is to suffer, to be loved
is to cause suffering.*

—Comtesse Diane

Friendship, Love & Laughter

*He who has learned
how to laugh at himself
shall never cease
to be entertained.*

—John Powell

Love is
the tie that blinds.

Friends are like melons.
Shall I tell you why?
To find one good,
you must a hundred try.

—Claude Mermet

Friendship, Love & Laughter

*Listlessness and silence
denote the lover.*

—Latin proverb

Friendship, Love & Laughter

*Happiness
is the only thing
that multiplies by
division.*

Friendship, Love & Laughter

You can't buy love,
but you can pay
heavily for it.

*Friends do not live
in harmony, as some say,
but in melody.*

—Henry David
Thoreau

Friendship, Love & Laughter

*Some pray to marry the
man they love,
my prayer will some-
what vary:
I humbly pray to Heaven
above
that I love the man
I marry.*

—Rose Stokes

Friendship, Love & Laughter

*Of all
the things God created,
I am often most grateful
He created laughter.*

—Charles Swindoll

Friendship, Love & Laughter

*I have noticed
that folks are generally
about as happy
as they have made up
their minds to be.*

—Abraham Lincoln

Friendship, Love & Laughter

*A friend
is one before whom
I may think aloud.*

—Emerson

Friendship, Love & Laughter

*Love does not
demand its own way.
It is not irritable
or touchy. It does not
hold grudges and will
hardly even notice
when others do it wrong.*

—1 Corinthians 13:5,6

Friendship, Love & Laughter

*A joy that's shared
is a joy made double.*

Friendship, Love & Laughter

*Love is the
triumph of imagination
over intelligence.*

—H.L. Mencken

*A friend
at one's back
is a safe bridge.*

—Dutch proverb

Friendship, Love & Laughter

*There is no fear
in love; but perfect love
casts out fear.*

—John 4:18 (NKJV)

Friendship, Love & Laughter

*He who tickles himself
may laugh when he pleases.*

—German proverb

*Love is the only game
that is not called
on account of darkness.*

—Thomas Carlyle

*A true friend
walks in when the
rest of the world
walks out.*

Friendship, Love & Laughter

*There are
three things that remain—
faith, hope, and love—
and the greatest of these
is love.*

—1 Corinthians 13:13

Friendship, Love & Laughter

*Laughter
is the closest thing
to the grace of God.*

—Karl Barth

*Age does not
protect you from love.
But love, to some extent,
protects you from age.*

—Jeanne Moreau

Friendship, Love & Laughter

Make new friends,
but don't forget
the old ones.

—Yiddish proverb

*'Tis better
to have loved and lost
than never to have
loved at all.*

—Alfred Lord Tennyson

Friendship, Love & Laughter

*Laughter is the
sun that drives winter
from the human face.*

—Victor Hugo

Friendship, Love & Laughter

*God
is the Creator
of laughter that is good.*

*A friend
is a person who
goes around saying
nice things about you
behind your back.*

*There is only
one kind of love,
but there are
a thousand
different versions.*

—La Rochefoucauld

Friendship, Love & Laughter

*Laugh,
if you are wise.*

—Latin proverb

Friendship, Love & Laughter

*Love is an
itch around the heart
that you can't scratch.*

Friendship, Love & Laughter

To a friend's house
the road is never long.

—Dutch proverb

*The heart that loves
is always young.*

Friendship, Love & Laughter

*A little levity
will save many
a good heavy thing
from sinking.*

—Samuel Butler

*Falling in love
is awfully simple,
but falling out of love
is simply awful.*

Friendship, Love & Laughter

*Faithful are the wounds of
a friend, but the kisses of
an enemy are deceitful.*

— Proverbs 27:6 (NKJV)

Friendship, Love & Laughter

*Love is an act
of endless forgiveness,
a tender look
which becomes a habit.*

—Peter Ustinov

Friendship, Love & Laughter

*If you're not allowed
to laugh in heaven,
I don't want to go there.*

—Martin Luther

Friendship, Love & Laughter

*Love at first sight
is possible,
but it always pays
to take a second look.*

Friendship, Love & Laughter

*It is the friends
you can call up
at 4 a.m. that matter.*

—Marlene Dietrich

Friendship, Love & Laughter

*Nothing raises man
to such noble peaks
nor drops him into such
ashpits of absurdity as the
act of falling in love.*

—Ridgely Hunt

Friendship, Love & Laughter

A hearty laugh
gives one a dry-cleaning,
while a good cry
is a wet wash.

Friendship, Love & Laughter

*I want to
make people laugh—
so they will begin
to see things seriously.*

—William Zinser

Friendship, Love & Laughter

*If two people
who love each other
let a single instant wedge
itself between them,
it grows—
it becomes a month,
a year, a century;
it becomes too late.*

—Jean Giraudoux

Friendship, Love & Laughter

*Love, you know,
seeks to make happy
rather than to be happy.*

—Ralph Connor

Friendship, Love & Laughter

*I like the laughter
that opens the lips
and the heart,
that shows at the same time
pearls and the soul.*

—Charles E. Jones

Friendship, Love & Laughter

*Love is the only
kind of fire which is
never covered by
insurance.*

*Three men
are my friends.
He that loves me,
he that hates me,
he that is indifferent to me.
Who loves me
teaches me tenderness.
Who hates me
teaches me caution.
Who is indifferent to me
teaches me self-reliance.*

—Parin

Friendship, Love & Laughter

Where there is great love
there is great pain.

Friendship, Love & Laughter

*Absence
does not make
the heart grow fonder,
but it sure heats up
the blood.*

—Elizabeth Ashley

*A man in love
shows great ingenuity
in making a fool
of himself.*

Friendship, Love & Laughter

*The only way
to have a friend
is to be one.*

Friendship, Love & Laughter

*Love is, above all,
the gift of oneself.*

—Jean Anouilh

Friendship, Love & Laughter

He who laughs
frightens away his
problems.

*Love is
merely a madness.*

—William Shakespeare

Friendship is like Rome.
It's not built in a day.

—Franklin P. Jones

Friendship, Love & Laughter

*Absence sharpens love,
presence strengthens it.*

—Thomas Fuller

Friendship, Love & Laughter

He who laughs, lasts.

—Mary Pettibone Poole

Friendship, Love & Laughter

*Love may not
make the world go round,
but it sure makes
the trip worthwhile.*

*Friendship improves
happiness and abates
misery by doubling our
joy and dividing our grief.*

—Joseph Addison

*Love is like the measles—
all the worse when it
comes late in life.*

—Douglas Jerrold

Friendship, Love & Laughter

*A hug is a roundabout
way of expressing
affection.*

Friendship, Love & Laughter

*Lovers always think
that other people have had
their eyes put out.*

—Spanish proverb

Friendship, Love & Laughter

It is not so much our friends' help that helps us as the confident knowledge that they will help us.

—Epicurus

Friendship, Love & Laughter

Love is the glue
that cements friendships.
Jealousy keeps it from
sticking.

Friendship, Love & Laughter

The curve of a smile
can set a lot of things
straight.

*Everyone likes a man
who can laugh at his
own expense.*

—John Lubbock